Contents

Introduction

I wonder if you picked up this book initially because the title grabbed you? I wonder if you smiled at the idea of child-initiated writing? I think we can all think of several children in our care who would rather, and indeed do, run a mile rather than write! Does the idea of these children coming willingly to a writing activity seem incredulous?

Some of the ideas in this book will need support and guidance initially. As with most, if not all, early years activities, children have to be shown how to use the resources first. But it will not be long before they are not only able to manage the activity by themselves but adapt and extend it, as well as clear away after it. Wherever possible and appropriate, have resources readily accessible so that children can set up activities themselves with minimal support and thus enable their writing to be truly child-initiated.

Learning to write takes several years, lots of patience and much perseverance. This book is about finding ways, lots of different ways, to make that long process fun and productive for both the child and practitioner. However throughout the book there are also ideas for taking the writing process further for those children who are well on their way to reaching the Early Learning Goals for writing and now need further consolidation of their writing skills.

I have also included case studies where relevant, that demonstrate how using this holistic approach facilitates learning across more than one area of learning. While practising a particular writing skill our children can also be learning and practising other skills.

I sometimes think that in this country, with the pressure of government targets, writing levels and SATS, we do make heavy weather of learning to write. Teaching a child to be a fluent writer is going to take several years so why spend several years miserably when we can actually spend that time pleasurably and purposefully?

Children need to see that even the adults in their setting can enjoy time doodling and enjoying the colour and texture of different media without feeling defined by outcome. The process of writing should be enjoyable and exciting but can be thwarted if there is the undue pressure of a desired outcome. Sometimes we need to remind ourselves that we are human beings not human 'becomings'. We need to allow the children in our care to simply 'be' – enjoying the stage they are at and not worrying about and planning for the next stage and what they will become. As Carlina Rinaldi says in her book In Dialogue with Reggio Emilia:

'We don't talk about preparing children for the future; it is the present that is important. We do not know what the future holds. Childhood is the best time of life, it should be enjoyed.'

We are all writers even if the writing that we produce does not resemble the work of an award winning published writer. We are all writers and our writing should be enjoyed and celebrated.

Our children also need to experience 'non writing' writing. Writing does not have to happen in formal, sitting down with paper and pen, situations. There are many exciting, multi-sensory media in which we can write; writing in strawberry blancmange paste is very therapeutic for a hot and bothered teacher as well as his/her hot and bothered pupil! And which letter formations are you more likely to remember; those made laboriously over your teacher's 'yellow writing' in your exercise book or those made freely with your own finger in a blue tray with a shallow covering of cool pink strawberry scented paste?

Writing does not have to be and, indeed, should not always be permanent. Many children want to be able to wipe away their writing or watch it evaporate in front of their very eyes.

As their writing disappears so do any imperfections and many children welcome that.

Disappearing writing takes on a magical quality as does 'magic writing' (see page 12) with resistance materials such as wax crayons and paint. Making writing magical can only entice children to want to write more!

Some practitioners may be concerned about the mess involved in these activities and also that resources may be wasted. I cannot say that these are not messy activities as many of them are, but I have successfully done most of these activities indoors with well-covered carpets, spill-able pots placed in larger trays and with minimum adult supervision. Most also lend themselves well to being outdoor activities.

We have to learn to supervise from a distance, allowing the children autonomy to have a go at mixing their own paints, for instance, and learning from their own mistakes. Putting smaller amounts of paint powder into smaller tubs, which the children can handle easily, helps.

Small yogurt pots can be used for paint powder and empty liquid soap dispensers are perfect for adding water.

7

A large picture instruction poster on the wall regarding the amount of powder to water required and the basics of colour mixing allows the children to take control. Then leave them to experiment, only helping out if asked or if absolutely necessary. Give lots of praise. For the first week this will be more time consuming than merely mixing the paint yourself but gradually the effort will be well worth it. As the children learn how to do the task you will notice their language use and interactions increasing and becoming more complex. They will learn about how materials change according to the amount of water added, how colours can be mixed and they will generally become more active learners.

Some of you may be reluctant to introduce such child-led learning. We are changing long held views on what is appropriate practice but in doing so we are working towards best practice where our children are active learners and confident in initiating their own learning. In order

to do this, we must empower them to access the resources in our settings. Equally, we must empower all of our colleagues to allow the children to have a go and not worry when mistakes and spills occur. Children learn as much, if not more, from their mistakes. They should be allowed to regard spills and errors as merely part of the learning process in a relaxed and happy setting and not anything to be concerned about. If we make a mess, we clean it up, no problem.

Children learning to write, or indeed learning anything, in a relaxed and happy environment will learn more quickly and be better able to build upon that foundation stage learning later on.

In order to facilitate a learning environment that best supports child-initiated writing, a checklist is included at the end of each chapter for practitioners to consider as a team. This checklist features key questions to promote discussion and to be used as a basis for future planning.

Writing using multi-sensory media

Writing in the early years is of course synonymous with mark making and finger painting.

'Writing' covers all aspects of mark making and finger painting is really finger writing. Finger painting is the first step in mark making. We often see young babies 'writing' in food spillages on their high chair table and looking quite surprised and pleased with themselves as they see the results of their efforts. Meal times can then become an even more protracted affair!

Finger writing can be enjoyed by very young children who find it difficult to hold a writing implement and by older children who enjoy the freedom from having to control pen, pencil or brush. It helps to build finger strength and enhances fine motor skills but also offers an additional dimension – for many children nothing can be more exciting than the deliciously tactile experience of paint (or whatever media is used) squelching through their fingers!

For this reason, expect little distinguishable mark making in the first few sessions, as many children will initially explore the medium before actually using it to make marks.

Over the years I have learnt that some children are frightened of making mistakes – sad but true. Writing in this kind of media can easily be erased by the writer if they are not pleased with the result. This can build confidence in these children to simply 'have a go' and when you feel that the time is right you can gently praise their efforts. 'What a shame you rubbed that out, I thought it was brilliant/so clever etc. I wonder if you could write it again to show your friends? I bet they'll love it too.'

9

Comments casually made with no pressure, as you are gently pottering in the same media or seemingly busy doing something else, can spur a child on to further 'work' and progress with no hint of correcting his or her work or any judgement having been made. We can all thrive in a relaxed learning environment!

The media described in this chapter are often messy and will need to be contained. You may wish children to wear aprons, which should be roomy and easy for the children to put on themselves, with some help from a friend, to encourage independence.

Suitable containers would be a water tray, sand tray, or builder's tray but these can be expensive and are often already being used by the setting for another activity. Baking trays offer a cheap alternative as do brightly coloured cat litter trays (brand new and unused of course!). I have had most success using cat litter trays as they fit neatly on a table, can accommodate one or two children's play and are light enough and safe enough for children to handle, carry and clean up when setting up or tidying away.

Exciting writing media

Flavoured blancmange

The children I worked with tended to prefer flavoured blancmange, especially strawberry, because it has a vibrant colour and is strongly scented. The activity therefore appeals to all of the senses, which can be discussed as they play.

Sprinkle a small amount (about two tablespoons) of blancmange powder into a tray. Add water (a spoonful at a time) and mix to form a stiff paste. Add a little more water so that you can finger write your name fairly easily but leave a trail so that the tray can be seen underneath. During the session you may need to add small quantities of water as the consistency does tend to thicken over time. Encourage the children to do this with you so you can discuss change – how the powder becomes a thick paste after mixing it with water and how the consistency can be changed.

Some children may not have eaten blancmange so this could be made and tasted as an extension activity.

Shaving foam

Add a light spray of shaving foam to the tray. Shaving foam has more 'wow' factor than shaving gel as the foam tends to float in wisps as the children play. Encourage the children to draw in the foam – smiley faces, houses, pets, favourite toys etc. Can they write the first letter of their name? You can encourage this in a relaxed atmosphere by simply drawing your own pet, writing your own name in the foam and saying what you are doing. Most children will do similarly, not just to please you but to prove that they can do it too!

Expect a lot of excited squeals with this activity and aprons are a must!

Case study

Jack rarely spoke to the children or practitioners in his group. When he first started at nursery he had spoken but the children found it difficult to understand him. No one had been unkind to him but Jack had been embarrassed. He seemed to resign himself to the fact that it was easier to say little or nothing at all and rely on gesture and body language than to try to enter into further verbal communication.

The practitioners at the setting became more and more concerned that Jack was engaging in behaviours similar to those of an elective mute. One morning the nursery teacher, Mrs. Johnson asked Jack to help her to set up a writing activity.

'What would you like to write with today?' she asked pointing to the various packs of blancmange, paints, shaving foam etc on the shelf.

Jack picked up the shaving foam and pointed to the writing trays for Mrs. Johnson to carry to the writing table with him.

'I wonder if anyone else would like to play with us?' Mrs. Johnson asked in a slightly louder tone, knowing that she would have several volunteers offering to join her and Jack!

Jack smiled at the other children and joined in as they all helped each other into their aprons. 'Thanks Jack' said Ben giving a thumbs up sign. Jack returned the thumbs up and grinned.

The children started by just feeling the foam. 'Oooh it's all soft and lovely.' 'It's bubbly.' 'My Dad's got this stuff at home, he does this,' and Lucy put the foam on her chin. The children shrieked with laughter, looking towards the practitioner to see if this 'is allowed'. Mrs. Johnson smiled and said that Lucy looked like Father Christmas. The children found this highly amusing and several of them also put the foam on their chins. In their excitement wisps of the foam were floating about them. With everyone's attention diverted by the wisps and the excitement enveloping the Father Christmases perhaps Jack's perceived pressure to talk and to be seen to be talking, lifted somewhat. Anyway, he started chattering away maybe to himself, maybe to the other children. 'Bubbles, bubbles,' he repeated as he scooped up the foam in his hands and threw it in the air. 'Mrs. Johnson, Jack is talking!' gasped one of the children. 'Of course', said Mrs. Johnson as nonchalantly as she could, smiling. 'Course!' said Jack busily, not even looking up.

I have done the same activity with young children who have no language but while doing the activity they have made gurgles, sounds and exclamations of pleasure. Reaffirming these sounds, commenting on their play writing progress, without any pressure of expectation of a reply, is probably the best course of action by the practitioner. A reciprocal, if non verbal, language exchange can be an enjoyable communication experience and meanwhile the children can build fine motor skills as well as language skills and an awareness of writing.

Activities such as shaving foam offer such wow factor and the children become so absorbed in what they are doing, that they can overcome barriers such as speech and social interaction issues, which may have seemed impossible. Holistic multi-sensory teaching and learning really does offer opportunities to practise several learning outcomes at the same time.

Of course some children do not enjoy messy activities and this should be accepted and understood. This is discussed further alongside the case study about Sam in Chapter Two.

Sand

Add sand – coloured or plain to the tray. This can provide a quieter writing experience than can be offered by the larger classroom sand tray. Other media can be mixed in such as coloured glitter to make it more exciting.

Icing sugar

Icing sugar (or flour) can be added to the tray to depict snow and link with weather related topics. Again water can be added to alter consistency. When weather permits, you could add real snow, which, again offers a discussion opportunity about how things change when warmed and can then be re-frozen, as well as offering mark-making experiences.

Traditional finger painting

Finger painting is easy and uncomplicated and offers opportunities for the children to learn more about colour mixing. When the children help you to mix the paint colours, limit the palette to the primary colours and suggest they try to make more colours from the red, yellow, and blue already mixed. Use a thick consistency of paint and either 'paint' in the tray or on art paper or rolls of lining paper. Add sand or glitter to the paint to get additional texture.

'Magic writing' – resistance writing inspires resistant writers!

Use a resistance media (white wax crayon or a white pastel stick) to write a message, a child's name, a smiley face etc. on white art paper. Encourage children to mix their own colour palette to colour wash the paper in their favourite colours – the resistance material does not take up the colour wash and the message/name is thus revealed. Young children find this very exciting – be prepared to have to do this many many times!

These tactile media can also be used to explore pattern, shape, size and position.

Taking it further

Older children who are working on the intricacies of correct letter formation will also benefit from working in tactile media rather than on paper. This finger writing is more relaxed than holding a writing tool which can often make young fingers ache after a short while. Consequently, children are more likely to stay at the activity much longer. I have actually timed these activities against pen and paper ones and a child's perseverance is considerably greater when tactile media is used! Mistakes are easily wiped away and the fluidity of the media allows a greater flow in the writing.

Once a child has perfected the formation of a particular letter using tactile media and you want written evidence of this accomplishment, then just one row of the letter, written correctly and independently in the child's writing book, is far better than rows and rows of poor, much corrected efforts shakily written over the teacher's yellow writing.

Writing on laminated pages

Laminated pages will have a limited life span and will need replacing every few months. However in the meantime, occasional cleaning with a whiteboard cleaner will extend their life and make them more inviting to use. It's a good idea to rotate their use anyway ensuring that you remove less popular pages and regularly offer new pages to maintain interest. File less popular pages away as what may not appeal to one cohort of children can be an instant success with another group. I used to include a new page or two every Monday. The children soon got used to this and used to immediately go to see what was new for them to write on. Gradually they even began to bring in their own pages for me to laminate for them. Though I did have to carefully consider the suitability of a few items, on the whole these contributions were very welcome and I was thrilled that parents and children felt they were involved and that they could contribute.

Window writing

Window writing using whiteboard marker pens is also exciting as it offers the 'wow' factor of an activity not usually allowed at home! Children need to be advised of the appropriateness of this and how we can write on the windows at school with these special marker pens but that this is not possible at home. Remember to test a small inconspicuous space first to make sure that you can clean the marker pen off completely!

If window writing is a success then you can buy window pens, which last longer. These will offer a more permanent display but will need a specific cleaning agent recommended by the pen manufacturer. Again check, on an inconspicuous area of window, that they can be removed eventually!

Taking it further

Older children who are learning to read and write the Reception High Frequency Words will enjoy the novelty of window writing. Using a whiteboard marker, write a starter sentence on the window based on the words you are currently working on e.g. Look, I can see… Invite the children to read the words, draw what they can see and then label the drawing. Some children will be able to copy and complete the sentence as well as add a relevant drawing e.g. Look, I can see a car.

As with all writing we practitioners can easily make this a chore without meaning to and thus break the spell of the 'wow' factor. So start with small steps; for the very young these may be doodles, older children may prefer to do a drawing and label before moving on to the complete sentence. Encourage the children to leave each other's writing on the window as they add their own. A window full of 'Look, I can see…' writing shows everyone that we are a class of writers, that we celebrate each other's writing and that we are also noticing the world around us!

wipe-away writing

Some children are more comfortable with their writing if they can instantly wipe away what they are not proud of – so wipe-away writing can have an important place in children's writing. Other children love the 'magic' aspect of writing that can just disappear with the wipe of a hand.

Provide whiteboards – individual and wall mounted – and maker pens with erasers and cloths for wiping away.

See also 'writing on laminated pages' on page 15.

Outdoor water painting

It is the temporary aspect of this writing that makes 'painting' outdoors with water so popular. Mark making with water cannot be seen so clearly and so any 'mistakes' the writer feels he or she may have made will soon evaporate anyway.

Water painting also appeals to children who enjoy making large movements in their writing and do not like to be confined to a piece of paper! Water is not as messy as paint either so some children who may feel a little clumsy with paint spills may be more at ease with outdoor water painting.

On rainy days water won't be needed as the children can 'write' on the wet windows.

Key questions

Writing using multi-sensory media can easily be incorporated into your daily planning rather than kept as special one off activities. The following questions may help you and your colleagues to think about the best way of incorporating multi-sensory media resources into each day's writing activities.

- Are all practitioners happy and relaxed about messy play and its contribution to writing? Do we have a shared understanding of how tactile media will contribute to our children's writing progress?

- Have we taken time to experience the different media ourselves discussing creative and non-creative mess? What is needed to ensure writing progress as well as ensuring some free time for the children to play in the media?

- Do all practitioners, parents and carers value tactile media? Do any of our colleagues, parents, or carers only value writing that has been done with paper and pen? Do we need to consider further training?

- Are aprons readily available at child height and can the children put these on independently or with the help of a friend?

- Are resources set out so that children can readily manage their messy play? Are cleaning materials readily and safely available? Have the children been shown how to tidy up after themselves and are they encouraged to do this after every session ready for the next person to use?

- Are any of our children nervous about getting messy or dirty? Will any of them need additional support or collaborative adult play until they feel more comfortable about joining in?

- Do any of our children have known allergies? Do we have a supply of non-allergenic gloves readily available? Have we discussed their use with parents of children with known allergies and do we have a list of suitable alternative activities for these children? Do we consider it necessary to obtain parental permission for use of some of these media?

Links with Early Learning Goals

Personal, Social and Emotional Development

- Continue to be interested, excited and motivated to learn.

Communication, Language and Literacy

- Link sounds to letters, naming and sounding the letters of the alphabet.
- Use their phonic knowledge to write simple regular words and make phonetically plausible attempts at more complex words.
- Explore and experiment with sounds, words and texts.
- Know that print carries meaning and, in English, is read from left to right and top to bottom.
- Write their own names and other things such as labels and captions, and begin to form simple sentences, sometimes using punctuation.
- Use a pencil and hold it effectively to form recognisable letters, most of which are correctly formed.

Problem Solving, Reasoning and Numeracy

- Talk about, recognise and recreate simple patterns.
- Use language such as 'circle' or 'bigger' to describe the shape and size of solids and flat shapes.
- Use everyday words to describe position.

Knowledge and Understanding of the World

- Investigate objects and materials by using all of their senses as appropriate.
- Look closely at similarities, differences, patterns and change.

Creative Development

- Respond in a variety of ways to what they see, hear, smell, touch and feel.
- Explore colour, texture, shape, form and space in two or three dimensions.

Writing without pens or pencils

Chapter one looked at mark making and writing using multi-sensory media. The best practice in Early Years teaching and learning naturally involves a multi-sensory holistic approach; which will accommodate all learning styles. The activities covered in chapter one will appeal to young children and offer the 'wow' factor. They are also fairly messy and will require some supervision at least until the children have understood how to handle the media and your expectations!

The activities in this chapter still offer multi-sensory approaches, but with slightly less messy materials. If your practitioner team is nervous about messy play or believes productive writing can only be formed with pens and pencils then the activities in this chapter may be a good starting point for you and your setting.

The activities here are still a little bit different; they involve fun tactile play that is less messy but children will still be learning important writing skills. Whilst not wanting our practice to be led by inspections and professional development observations, we do need to demonstrate that we are teaching and our children are learning via informal multi-sensory approaches.

Writing with string, wool and spaghetti!

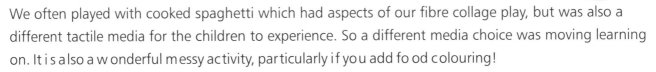

In our settings we all have craft materials which lend themselves well to letter formation. Indeed, whilst working on collage with wool, string and threads children often notice that the length of fibre has fallen into a shape resembling a letter in their name and point this out.

We often played with cooked spaghetti which had aspects of our fibre collage play, but was also a different tactile media for the children to experience. So a different media choice was moving learning on. It is also a wonderful messy activity, particularly if you add food colouring!

As briefly mentioned in Chapter One you need to be aware that some children dislike messy play sometimes to the point of phobia. These children should never be coerced, cajoled or coaxed into messy play. However, they should see what is happening and how the other children are enjoying the activity. That way they can come to see messy play for what it is – lots of fun and totally non-threatening. They must also learn that while nursery/school has some rules that must be kept to ensure a safe and happy environment, we all have choices and our likes/dislikes and feelings generally will never be dismissed or ignored.

I do like children to experience as many of the activities that I set out as possible as I then feel that they have indeed enjoyed a 'broad and balanced curriculum'. But children can experience the activity by simply observing, which is what many do with particular types of play that they are unfamiliar with or uncertain of.

In the following case study I don't think we, as practitioners, considered the play to be particularly messy. We had played with far worse in previous sessions! But for Sam this was most definitely messy to the point of causing him distress.

Sam disliked messy play. He hated having dirty hands whether the dirt was sand, paint, glue or even food; he became extremely upset and had to wash his hands immediately. His distress was painful to see and temper tantrums followed very quickly if he wasn't able to wash immediately.

One day I was playing with the children with a tray of cooked spaghetti. First of all we 'squished and squashed' our hands through the slimy mixture. Shrieks of 'Mrs. Clere it's all gooey' and 'We had this for tea, last night Mrs. Clere' and 'Look mine's like a worm!' drew a lot of attention from the other children in the room. Sam was no exception. I noticed that he had stopped playing with the cars and garage (a safe game as he perceived this to be entirely free from any chance of getting dirty) and that he had stood up to watch. I invited some of the other children to join us but deliberately didn't extend the invitation to Sam. I noticed that gradually he came forward and after about ten minutes was standing next to me.

By this time the children had decided that the spaghetti was indeed a tray of worms and had started to lay strands of spaghetti along side each other to work out whose was the longest. I started to introduce some math's language – long, longer, longest, short, shorter, shortest. Sam enjoyed maths and became even more interested in the activity. As we compared our 'worms' I began to label mine as 'Mrs. Clere's and Sam's worm' Sam smiled.

As interest began to wane a little I suggested that we could change the colour of our worms by adding some food colouring. 'What colour would you like the worms to be, Sam?' I asked. 'Green', he whispered. So Sam had the task of fetching and adding the food colouring which the rest of us mixed in. I took one spaghetti worm out of the trough and began to sing, 'There's a worm at the bottom of the garden' and some children joined in and others continued to play with the spaghetti in the tray. On the palm of my hand I arranged the spaghetti into an 'S' and said to Sam – 'Look now the worm is in the shape of the first letter in your name' 'And the first letter of spaghetti!' he grinned. At that stage Sam knew most of the alphabet letters, could make a clear link between phonemes (letter sounds) and the corresponding grapheme (written letter) and was beginning to read some of the simpler books on the nursery bookshelf. I thought that perhaps I could use his knowledge of letters and his pride in his early reading to overcome some of his issues with messy play.

I stretched the spaghetti into a long line and said, 'Now what letter can I make?' After two or three letters I claimed to be stuck and asked for help making the letters and seconds later Sam was playing with the spaghetti, albeit just one strand but for him this was progress! I pre-empted any horror at dirty hands by suggesting we all washed our hands together as our hands were now a little green and we would make everything we touched green. Some adventurous children touched their faces and ran to the mirror squealing with glee at their green reflections!

Later in the morning, Sam led me to the spaghetti tray and together we played 'worm writing'.

Over the next few months Sam did begin to enjoy some messy play. By the time he left nursery for the reception class his phobia had eased somewhat; his distress subsided and tantrums were a thing of the past. He voluntarily engaged in many aspects of messy play knowing that he could withdraw at any time and he could always wash his hands whenever he wished. I don't think Sam is ever likely in the near future to put messy play at the very top of his favourite activities but he did enjoy some messy play and he no longer felt the huge upset that he had originally suffered from.

Whilst I had been trying to engage reluctant writers with messy play I had in fact engaged a child reluctant to engage in messy play by using his interest in maths and letters.

Moulds, templates and stencils

Filling alphabet moulds with sand, jelly or coloured, bubbled or scented water will help to strengthen hands and fingers improving fine motor skills. This activity is pleasingly tactile and can help those children who find the actual physical process of writing difficult. Activities that include such experiential play can also help those children with speech and communication problems.

collage writing

I often find that children who are interested in writing and the written word; the finished product and its purpose, are not yet ready to actually write for themselves. Similarly, whilst many children are not bothered whether or not their writing resembles an adult's writing or that found in a storybook, others are acutely aware that their writing is not readily understood and grow tired of translating it. I have become embarrassingly aware that it is usually well meaning adults who ask for translation whereas children are often very accepting of their peer's hieroglyphic script.

It would therefore seem reasonable to provide opportunities to write which do not necessarily require pen, paper and the ability to form recognisable print. Collage writing fulfils this remit. Children can use pre-printed fonts and scripts, cutting and sticking the letters to form words or use other materials to form their own letters. Either way a writing collage is formed.

Resources ideas for collage writing

- A variety of different papers – printer paper, coloured paper, envelopes, off-cuts of card etc.

- A selection of printed scripts in a variety of fonts – these can be printed from the computer, or be from magazine and newspaper pages. Try to offer print that is both upper and lower case and in a variety of colours, as children notice and will comment on differences and similarities. This can offer opportunities for discussion of fonts and consolidation of colour knowledge.

- Other media can be used to form letters rather than actual letters themselves e.g. coloured mosaic paper squares, string, wool, thread, sand, sugar, glitter, rice, uncooked pasta etc.

- Stickers.

- Glue

    o White liquid glue – messy but fun! Very young children will play with the glue initially rather than actually use it for their sticking project. Please let them play with the glue – they are learning what makes glue, glue; what its properties are and what it can do. Without this initial exploration stage a vital learning stage has been ignored.

    o Glue stick – not so messy and very easy for young children to use independently.

    o Home-made glue – traditional flour and water paste is worth mixing now and again.

Note: Please let children help you to mix paints and glue! It's a much slower process, of course, but they will learn about how materials (in this case the flour or paint powder) can be changed by adding water. As we work with young children we need to be aware of all the learning opportunities there are throughout the day, even in the preparation of our resources. The children will have ownership of their work if they have chosen what to use and they will learn a lot in the process of mixing the paint colours etc. We need to see that the process of a project is as important, if not more important than the end result. We are on a learning journey where the final destination is only a part of the overall learning.

Collage writing but without the glue

Items readily found in an early years setting can also be used to form letters and write words e.g. pine cones, counters, trucks and cars, shells, etc. These are easily dismantled by the children when they no longer want them on display or want to change what they have 'written'.

The children in a reception class were encouraged to bring into school their favourite traditional stories and one child brought in Hansel and Gretel. After sharing the story some of the children set up the house and woods outdoors and walked into the woods scattering breadcrumbs as they went. At snack time they watched the birds eating some of the crumbs. One of the children suggested that Hansel and Gretel should have written, 'Help' in the crumbs so the children did that later in pebbles. Another child made a smiley face with her pebbles saying that was how she felt when the father comes to rescue Hansel and Gretel in the woods.

The children used a variety of natural materials and made lots of trails and patterns in the reception garden. As this activity had caught the children's imaginations, the following day the practitioners extended the activity by providing 2D biscuit houses to decorate with icing pens. They also provided 2D card houses for decoration with 3D paint pens, which were made into a story display board.

Plasticine writing

Given a piece of plasticine or dough to play with most children begin by moulding and stretching it into a worm-like length of stretchiness. This is then formed into many things; animals, flowers and, of course with maybe a little support, letters.

Clay, salt dough and air drying media make the final lettering permanent and can be decorated later with paint, glitter, sequins, paper and beads, varnished and used to decorate coat pegs, photo displays etc.

Try to use different moulding media as they have different properties and densities and are suitable for the different stages of fine motor skills. Soft play plasticine is less dense and more easily manipulated and thus more appropriate for very young children. Clay requires greater strength and is therefore more appropriate for those children with greater finger and hand strength.

Playing with these materials strengthens hand muscles, dexterity and control and will be invaluable when children begin to hold and manipulate writing tools. In the meantime, they offer the chance to 'write' in a relaxed and informal environment without the pressure to hold and manipulate a pencil, brush, crayon or felt tip correctly in order to mark make.

Similarly, construction toys such as lego can be used to 'write'. Reluctant writers (quite often boys) may enjoy writing with lego or with sticks and stones on a path in the setting's outdoor area.

Lucas, a child nearing the end of reception, was finding writing difficult and building words phonetically very difficult. Whilst his teacher wanted Lucas to extend his learning in this area, she did not want him to feel under any pressure. Lucas loved any play that involved vehicles, so his teacher decided to use this as a 'vehicle' for learning!

The learning intention for the week was onset and rime; building words that rhymed with 'at'. So she placed 'a' and 't' stickers on the side of the pick-up truck and letters that would make 'at' rhyming words such as 'b', 'c', 'f", 'h' etc. on to different coloured cars. Several children played the car towing game with Lucas forming the 'at' family words with the cars and the truck and reading them as they played.

Writing with plants

Children love to see their name, or the initial letter of their name, especially in unusual places. When sowing seeds consider sowing the seeds in the form of the child's name. Seed cress grown on tissue in the shape of a child's initial name letter is fun.

Similarly, if you are growing vegetables such as marrows, pumpkins or squash in the setting's garden consider carving a message: 'Hello', 'Smile', 'Look!' etc. in the skin of a young vegetable and as it grows, the message will also grow.

Bedding plants and bulbs can be planted to form the word 'Welcome' or 'Hello' or the setting's name. The children will enjoy pointing these words and letters out to parents and carers as they arrive in your setting each morning.

For instant 'indoor writing gardens' that the children can access themselves, buy some small tubs of mustard and cress from the supermarket (they cost about 25p per punnet) and divide them up into ten portions. Several of these can be used to 'write' letters in miniature tray gardens. They can be grown on for a few days or eaten the same day.

Taking it further

Towards the end of the reception year as children are beginning to recognise and match upper and lower case letters and their phonemes, a similar game can be played outside on the trikes and bikes. Set up two washing lines – one pegged with lower case letters and one with the corresponding upper case letters. Children cycle from line to line matching the letters as they go. Similarly, you could make parking the ride-on toys at tidy up time a game as the letter on a trikes 'number plate' can be matched to a letter on the parking space. If you decide to offer play opportunities such as these, it's important that children make the number plates and label the parking spaces themselves, as this gives them ownership of the activity and they are therefore more likely to use the facility and access the learning involved. Involving children more and more in the preparation of activities fires their imaginations and often provides us with opportunities to take our planning along valid tangents that we may not have thought of.

Encourage older children to write using letters, words and pictures they have cut out of magazines and newspapers. Help with the spelling and word building of simple CVC (consonant/vowel/consonant) words i.e. cat and high frequency words you are working towards. Children can also use collage letter notices and labels. They also demonstrate the children's input into the organisation of the setting.

Key questions

As writing with pens and pencils is the norm, using other tools and media will offer a different dimension to our writing activities. The following ideas will help you to consider a wider range of writing activities, situations that may arise and how you, as a setting, wish to consider your approach and generate an agreed working ethos.

- Are the resources easily accessible for the children to use independently? Are they attractively set out, well organized, well maintained and in sufficient numbers? Are they contributed to regularly in order to sustain interest and motivation?

- Do we see this as an important way of improving writing skills? Do we use the children's work in this area as evidence via photos, noting what they said during our observations? Do we formally include this area in our observations list?

- Do we encourage the children to use several different media together or do we try to keep certain media to certain areas for reasons of tidiness? Are we confining creativity?

- Can children move freely to different areas to use other materials, refer to books and things they have seen in other parts of the setting to improve their work or are they 'encouraged' to 'stay here and finish your work'.

- Do we have a problem solving ethos in our setting? Do we discuss our work, what we want to do next, discuss suggestions and solutions to difficulties? Do we as adults become offended if our solution is not tried or adopted?

- Have we considered practicalities – do we daily discard the dried up felt tips? Do we sharpen the pencils and crayons each day? Do the scissors cut all the papers we want them to cut? Does the glue really stick all the different paper and card weights we are expecting it to stick? There is nothing more frustrating than tools that do not do their job.

Links with Early Learning Goals

Personal, Social and Emotional Development

- Continue to be interested, excited and motivated to learn.
- Be confident to try new activities, initiate ideas and speak in a familiar group.
- Maintain attention, concentrate, and sit quietly when appropriate.
- Have a developing awareness of their own needs, views and feelings, and be sensitive to the needs, views and feelings of others.
- Form good relationships with adults and peers.
- Work as part of a group or class, taking turns and sharing fairly, understanding that there needs to be agreed values and codes of behaviour for groups of people, including adults and children, to work together harmoniously.
- Consider the consequences of their words and actions for themselves and others.
- Select and use activities and resources independently.
- Understand that people have different needs, views, cultures and beliefs that need to be treated with respect.
- Understand that they can expect others to treat their needs, views with respect.

Communication, Language and Literacy

- Interact with others, negotiating plans and activities and taking turns in conversation.
- Enjoy listening to and using spoken and written language, and readily turn to it in their play and learning.
- Sustain attentive listening, responding to what they have heard with relevant comments, questions or actions.
- Extend their vocabulary, exploring the meanings and sounds of new words.
- Speak clearly and audibly with confidence and control and show awareness of the listener.
- Link sounds to letters, naming and sounding the letters of the alphabet.
- Use their phonic knowledge to write simple regular words and make phonetically plausible attempts at more complex words.
- Explore and experiment with sounds, words and texts.
- Read a range of familiar and common words and simple sentences independently.

- Know that print carries meaning and, in English, is read from left to right and top to bottom.
- Write their own names and other things such as labels and captions, and begin to form simple sentences, sometimes using punctuation.
- Attempt writing for different purposes, using features of different forms such as lists, stories and instructions.

Problem Solving, Reasoning and Numeracy

- Talk about, recognise and recreate simple patterns.
- Use language such as 'circle' or 'bigger' to describe the shape and size of solids and flat shapes.
- Use everyday words to describe position.

Knowledge and Understanding of the World

- Investigate objects and materials by using all of their senses as appropriate.
- Look closely at similarities, differences, patterns and change.
- Select the tools and techniques they need to shape, assemble and join materials they are using.

Physical Development

- Handle tools, objects, construction and malleable materials safely and with increasing control.

Creative Development

- Respond in a variety of ways to what they see, hear, smell, touch and feel.
- Express and communicate their ideas, thoughts and feelings by using a widening range of materials, suitable tools, imaginative and role-play, movement, designing and making, and a variety of songs and musical instruments.
- Explore colour, texture, shape, form and space in two or three dimensions.

Writing our name:
a passport to literacy

Hall & Robinson (1995) talk of the empowerment children will hopefully experience when they learn to write. They discuss how the ability to write one's name has often been the measure by which a nation's literacy has been recorded. Thus 'the writing of one's own name has, for many hundreds of years, been seen as a rite of passage towards literate behaviour.'

Children often use the letters in their name to move from emergent writing and mark making to more formal writing. They will string together the letters from their name randomly but read those letters back to you as a complex sentence or story. At first this story may change with each reading but as time goes on it will be the same story. As stated in the Early Learning Goals, the child has begun to understand that text carries meaning and practitioners will realise that this is the very early stages. To anyone else, this is a string of random letters, albeit, those found in that particular child's name but to the writer they are a complete and meaningful text.

Not only will the child be learning that print carries meaning but also learn that the correct way to write English text is left to right, starting at the top of the page and progressing to the bottom. As they write they will be learning that they can write for different purposes too.

Thus learning to write one's name is very important and a gateway to learning further literacy skills. Some children are aware that writing is important and that a writer acquires some status.

Learning to write one's name for its own sake can be a laborious task. But if children are writing their name for a reason: to label their work, to send a card to a sick friend or write a party invitation then the process has purpose and meaning and most children aspire to make a good job of it.

29

One name, many different name cards

All children should have at least one name card readily accessible so that they can independently copy their name until such time when no prompt is needed. A starting dot and arrows, showing correct letter formation, can help as long as the children have had a little practice with an adult initially and know that these are merely aides and not a part of the letter itself!

Children should be encouraged to independently access their own name cards to label their work. There need to be several cards in different locations – at least one indoors and a laminated one outdoors. These should be made by the children with a little assistance to ensure accuracy so that when they later use them independently as prompts, they are not copying and reinforcing earlier mistakes.

When a child has copied their name from their name card, they will be very proud of what they have achieved. Be very wary of correcting letter formation at this stage. Choose your moment carefully and praise correctly formed letters before discussing those that need further practice. Be aware of a child's mood – today may not be the day to improve the letter 'a' but be assured that a child will almost certainly be learning something else of equal importance that day from sharing a particular toy, joining in a particular activity or even accessing their own name card and labeling their own work instead of expecting you to do it. Perhaps the correct formation of letter 'a' needs to wait another day.

To add interest, name cards can be written in various media e.g. sandpaper, glitter, collaged and laminated, computer or hand written and then hole punched and threaded.

Audio name cards

Making name cards especially in art/craft media appeal to those children who are visual or kinaesthetic learners. Audio name cards would be useful for those children who have more success accessing their learning via auditory means. Once recorded, store auditory name cards where they are easily accessed independently by the children and ensure that you have shown them how to use the class tape machine. Set some time aside to write the child's name with them, recording the instructions as you go. The name that you write together as you record on to the tape can be used as the tape cover. You can add a start dot and arrows to help with formation.

Here is an example of the recording. 'Hello Sam. Let's write your name. Let's write Sam. S-a-m. Let's start with the 'S' like a snake. Start at the top and go round like in a curly c and then let's give the 'S' snake a curly tail. Does your 'S' look like the one on the tape cover? Now let's write 'a'. Start at the top and go round and then up. Go down and then add a little flick. And now the 'm'. Start at the top, go down, up, over the bridge, down, over the bridge, down and add a little flick. Brilliant – you've written S-a-m; Sam, well done.'

You'll probably find only a few children will need this auditory prompt but several more will like the novelty!

When Kamal came to visit the reception class as part of an induction programme of visits his teacher asked him if he was looking forward to coming to school. 'Yes,' he said 'Cos then I'll be able to write like my sister in Mrs. Smith's class'. When Kamal later entered the reception class his teacher learnt just how much he admired his older sister – the greater freedoms she enjoyed (playing out with friends, later bedtime etc.) and her more advanced skills including being able to 'write properly' to which Kamal aspired.

Many children aspire to be like older siblings and writing their name is the first step and indeed the rite of passage that Nigel Hall and Anne Robinson write about.

Key questions

Throughout the day children will have many occasions when they need to be able to write their name; to label and identify their work and belongings or to show when they have experienced a learning activity for example. Therefore I have found that a formal sitting down name writing practice session really is not necessary.

- When children bring in treasured possessions from home do you take time to acknowledge their 'treasure' and its value and explain that it should be labelled to ensure safe-keeping. Do you take a little time to help the child to label the item with their name explaining how to write their name as you go? For example "Look there is an "S" at the beginning of your name "S for Sophie" etc. This is important because you are demonstrating that our writing does have a purpose.

- Can children readily access pre-cut labels on which they can write their names? Are these labels in a tray next to sharpened pencils, and other mark making materials? Are laminated name labels also nearby so that the children can copy their names?

- Do you take time to ensure that the children are labelling their work? Do you also write their name if they are having difficulty, writing with the child rather than after they have left an area?

- Do you value a child's name writing especially emergent mark making, celebrating it and also writing the child's name so that another adult can read the name; thus making the child feel that their mark making is successfully being read back?

- Do you have a special board to pin items that have not been named so that you can find its owner? Children will be upset if their work is lost and when it has been found you will be able to explain that their angst could have been avoided with a name label – again this is demonstrating that our writing does have a purpose.

- When a child can successfully write their first name do you go on to work on their surname, complementing their success thus far?

Personal, Social and Emotional Development

- Select and use activities and resources independently.

Communication, Language and Literacy

- Know that print carries meaning and, in English, is read from left to right.

- Write their own names and other things such as labels and captions, and begin to form simple sentences, sometimes using punctuation.

- Use a pencil and hold it effectively to form recognisable letters, most of which are correctly formed.

Knowledge and Understanding of the World

- Select the tools and techniques they need to shape, assemble and join materials they are using.

- Use information and communication technology to support their learning.

Writing on the run

The average under six year old (if there is such a person!) is a mobile being and that is how it should be. Sitting down quietly is an anathema, sitting down quietly to write seems unreasonable when you are so young. I find it difficult to teach children that their mark making has a purpose when I am not making it fit for their purpose but rather making their writing fit my purpose. I therefore feel that we have to adapt our writing opportunities to fit in with our children's 'busy-ness'. They need to be able to write on the run. To make jottings and take notes, and leave messages as they go. In order that they may do so effectively we need to offer writing stations that are mobile.

'It may be that some children prefer to read and write outside and get better results if they do.'
Outdoor Play In the Early Years Helen Bilton

Treasure hunts and message trails

Children love hide and seek. They love the joy of hiding objects and finding objects. Finding foam letters in jelly will encourage writing with the letters and mark making with the jelly. Other items can be hidden in other messy media.

Treasure hunts involving searching for the letters in our names, letter sounds and objects that begin with that sound and words that we are learning in our reading scheme, are more fun and more active than sitting down with paper, pen or a reading scheme book.

Similarly, a set of post-it notes and a pencil with a leader child and adult sticking clues on a treasure hunt or message trail is fun and inspires many children to want to write and to want to read. Initially these trails will need adult support. Discuss the number of clues and where you will put them.

Then you can offer a 'message prompts' clipboard to support the game with numbered picture or word clues for the children to copy and follow. Later the support board can offer ideas. Older children will be able to draw or write their own clues.

In its simplest form, a message trail can simply be a mark making follow me game where a child writes on a post-it note and sticks it on a tree, wall, bench and other children follow and have to copy the same pattern and stick it on the same tree, wall, bench etc.

Mobile writing stations

The problem with writing is that many practitioners see it as a sedentary occupation whereas most young writers are on the move; and this is why many children are reluctant to initiate the activity as they feel their movement may be curtailed.

The pure joy of movement can be seen in every early years settings from the baby who has just learnt to 'cruise' along the furniture clinging on for dear life to the rambunctious four year old hurling himself across the classroom to the resigned exclamations of 'walk' from the practitioner. It is hardly surprising then that for many young children writing just does not appeal, as they know that they will be required to sit still for what must feel like an extraordinarily long time.

Writing stations, which are dotted around the setting, easily accessed, and not requiring special equipment or seating could be the answer, as well as writing bags, boxes and trays which make writing a mobile activity that can be enjoyed anywhere. Have your own pencil case/special pen/journal which you carry round – not just to make observation notes but to actually take time out to enjoy mark making with your children.

Mobile writing stations such as trolleys, bags, boxes and trays enable children to add to the resources that have already been set up either by the practitioners or by the children. When children have ownership of the activity they tend to benefit more from the play.

Resource ideas for mobile writing stations

- Buckets with assorted brushes – label the buckets with a pictorial and written sign 'fill with water' and this bucket can be used outdoors for water painting walls and windows.

- Containers with lining/wall paper and border rolls, assorted large felt markers and wax crayons.

- Gardener's wheelbarrow with plant pots, seed packets, envelopes for DIY seed envelopes, crayons, pencils, plant labels, watering cans, pack of compost for digging area outdoors.

- Rewards box containing stickers, stars, blank labels, small pieces of card, paper and felt tips for making 'well done' stickers, certificate cards and scrolls.

- Push-along trolleys holding similar stationery found on the indoor and outdoor writing tables i.e. chalk, felt tips, pens, pencils, rubbers, rulers, hole punches, crayons, card, a variety of paper, tracing paper, lined, squared etc. stickers, stamps and ink pads.

- Children's novelty/character lunch boxes with handles or small plastic DIY tool boxes with carry handles holding a selection of stationery as above.

- Themed and novelty birthday cards and stationery (bought cheaply in pound shops or printed from the computer) to make up themed writing bags, a princess writing bag with fluffy trimmed pens and tiara, a builder's toolbox with measuring tape, toy hammers, screwdrivers, pencils, paper and hard hat, a doctor's/nurse's/vet's medicine bag with stethoscope, thermometer forehead strip, prescription pad and patient notes.

- A couple of easels dotted around your setting with paper set up and crayons or felt tips and paper set ready with a label 'Can you draw what you can see?' This may inspire some observational drawing and a written caption. Children will find this much easier to access independently than a painting easel.

- If your setting still has a formal registration time you will probably find that the children will love to have their own register. Set up a small register space in the setting – you will need a chair for the 'teacher', an A4 book with a list of the children's names on each page, and a pen. If you put all these in a basket with a handle then the register can be done anywhere in the setting. I usually put a storybook in the basket too as many children do register and story time together!

Trolleys can be pushed and pulled, emptied and filled. Bags and boxes can be filled and emptied. Trays can be filled, emptied and their contents arranged and re-arranged. This is what some children might choose to do with your carefully considered resources. Not a word may be written. Try not to be too disappointed! The children in your care may be working on particular development schemas i.e. trajectory, connecting, rotational, transporting, enveloping and containing, transformation and scattering and this is why they may play with the resources in a different way from what you intended.

Tina Bruce discusses schemas further in *Early Childhood Education*:

'Schemas are patterns of linked behaviours which the child can generalise and use in a whole variety of different situations. It is best to think of schemas as being a cluster of pieces which fit together.'

It's also important to realize that we provide resources as a starting point for our children's play. We may have a lesson plan with learning intentions that we want our children to be working towards but within our settings we are helping to create play scenarios with our children not for our children. And this includes our involvement in all areas of learning including writing.

Tina Bruce in Developing Learning in Early Childhood reminds us that *'All an adult needs to remember if the play is to be deep and rich in quality, is that their play agenda is no more important than that of the other players'*.

I sat down at the writing table one day to write myself a quick note to remind me that a child was being collected by a different family member that evening. As I put the post-it note in my pocket I asked a child at the writing table if he liked the new 'magic' felt tips which changed colour if you wrote on them with one of the pens. He said they were brilliant and invited me to have a go, telling me which were his favourite colours so I sat and experimented, soon attracting an interested crowd.

Conclusion

If you want your children to want to write, then they must see the benefits of writing. They must see that it has a purpose, but most of all they need to see that it is an enjoyable experience. You are the key to this.

It reminded me of Frank Smith's ideas in *The myths of writing* where he talks about what messages a teacher may be giving his/her children about writing.

'A teacher who is only seen writing comments on children's work, reports for parents or notes or exercises for classroom activities will demonstrate that writing is simply for administrative or class room purposes.' Frank Smith (1981) *The myths of writing* Language Arts Vol 58 pp 792-798:

This mark making for pleasure and recollecting Frank Smith's words reminded me to take time to enjoy mark making and writing for pleasure and to enjoy this with the children.

Writing for a purpose is an important part of our writing curriculum. Writing for pleasure should be an important part of our writing lives

Taking it further

Encourage the use of 'writing easels'. Peg several sheets of paper to the easel and attach different coloured marker pens so that they stay with the easel and are not taken elsewhere. Using bright colours makes the writing activity more appealing. Marker pens are easier for those children who may find gripping a pencil and pencil control difficult; Children can still make the marks with even a light grip and so most children can enjoy some success.

Offer starter sentences: What can you see?

Today I have…

My friend is…

You may need to offer picture cues and you will need to be close by, encouraging the children to 'have a go' at writing a response.

Key questions

Writing is traditionally considered to be a sedentary occupation. The following points may help you to ensure that quality writing is still taking place.

- Do the writing activities still offer valid writing opportunities? Can you offer more than just a notebook and pencil?

- Do the activities relate to what they are contained in e.g. gardening or building writing activities in a wheelbarrow?

- Do you regularly check that the writing resources are still within each writing station – are they in good condition?

- Are we encouraging the children to build stories and role-play scenarios around these writing resources? Do we talk to them in character; encouraging them to take on a role and write in that role?

- Are we offering sufficient support so that there is some writing on the run and not merely lots of running?!

Personal, Social and Emotional Development

- Continue to be interested, excited and motivated to learn.
- Be confident to try new activities, initiate ideas and speak in a familiar group.
- Maintain attention, concentrate and sit quietly when appropriate.
- Respond to significant experiences, showing a range of feelings when appropriate.
- Form good relationships with adults and peers.
- Work as part of a group or class, taking turns and sharing fairly, understanding that there needs to be agreed values and codes of behaviour for groups of people, including adults and children, to work together harmoniously.
- Understand what is right, what is wrong and why.
- Consider the consequences of their words and actions for themselves and others.
- Select and use activities and resources independently.

Communication, Language and Literacy

- Interact with others, negotiating plans and activities and taking turns in conversation.
- Enjoy listening to and using spoken and written language, and readily turn to it in their play and learning.
- Sustain attentive listening, responding to what they have heard with relevant comments, questions or actions.
- Listen with enjoyment, and respond to stories, songs and other music, rhymes and poems and make up their own stories, songs, rhymes and poems.
- Extend their vocabulary, exploring the meanings and sounds of new words.
- Speak clearly and audibly with confidence and control and show awareness of the listener.
- Use language to imagine and recreate roles and experiences.
- Use talk to organise, sequence and clarify thinking, ideas, feelings and events.
- Hear and say sounds in words in the order in which they occur.
- Explore and experiment with sounds, words and texts.
- Retell narratives in the correct sequence, drawing on language patterns of stories.

- Know that print carries meaning and, in English, is read from left to right and top to bottom.

- Show an understanding of the elements of stories, such as main character, sequence of events and openings, and how information can be found in non-fiction texts to answer questions about where, who, why and how.

- Attempt writing for different purposes, using features of different forms such as lists, stories and instructions.

- Write their own names and other things such as labels and captions, and begin to form simple sentences, sometimes using punctuation.

- Use a pencil and hold it effectively to form recognisable letters, most of which are correctly formed.

- Link sounds to letters, naming and sounding the letters of the alphabet.

- Use their phonic knowledge to write simple regular words and make phonetically plausible attempts at more complex words.

Problem Solving, Reasoning and Numeracy

- Say and use number names in order in familiar contexts.

- Count reliably up to ten everyday objects.

- Recognise numerals 1 to 9.

- Talk about, recognise and recreate simple patterns.

- Use everyday words to describe position.

Knowledge and Understanding of the World

- Look closely at similarities, differences, patterns and change.

- Select the tools and techniques they need to shape, assemble and join materials they are using.

Physical Development

- Handle tools, objects, construction and malleable materials safely and with increasing control.

Creative Development

- Respond in a variety of ways to what they see, hear, smell, touch and feel.

- Express and communicate their ideas, thoughts and feelings by using a widening range of materials, suitable tools, imaginative and role-play, movement, designing and making, and a variety of songs and musical instruments.

- Explore colour, texture, shape, form and space in two or three dimensions.

Writing opportunities within the daily routine

Each day, within our setting's routine there are many writing opportunities. Children see us writing and many will want to copy what we are doing. We have all been asked what we are doing when we fill in registers, observation post-it notes etc. Try to have a set of duplicate, child-friendly similar stationery for your children to use. An exercise book with the class list can instantly become a register. I am always surprised how children just love playing at being the teacher. Try to make such role-play opportunities as mobile as possible – an open basket entices the player more than a closed bag and if it has a carry handle it can be easily transported indoors or out. Flexible, plastic gardening trugs are very child friendly as they are light weight when empty and come in a variety of sizes. They are also very colourful and easy on restricted budgets. As you assess the children's use of free flow areas such as different role-play areas and the snack area, encourage the children to independently tick their name off against that activity once they have done it.

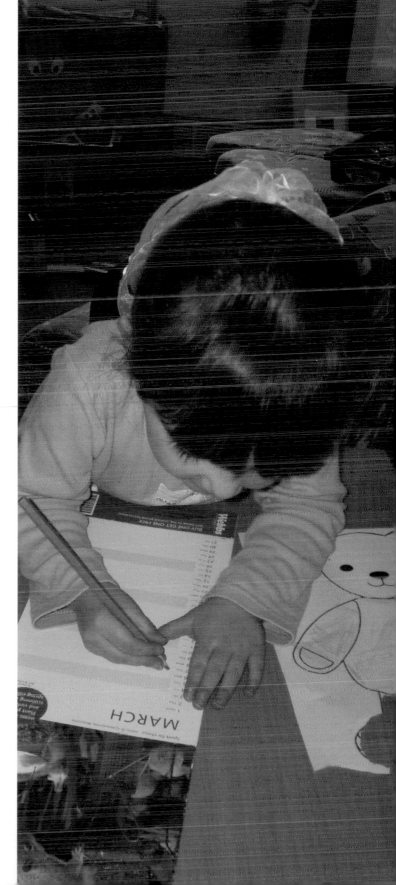

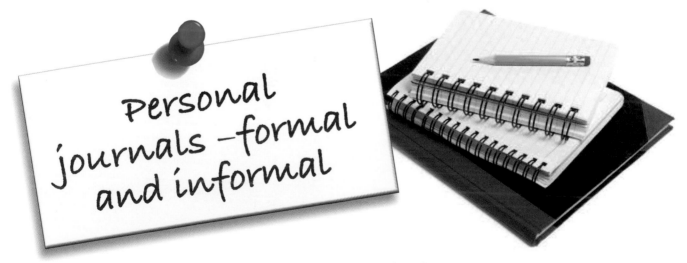

Encourage children to take photos of their day, which they can annotate in a nursery diary. Similarly, an assessment record of their stay in your setting can be a joint effort if both you and the child record observations of their experiences including photographs, artwork and writing.

A big book diary completed at the end of a teaching session with a photo and note of what has happened that day, written by children and practitioners, fascinates children and is often returned to as children find a sense of security in going back days later to 'read' what has happened before. For younger children, this is security in the sense of 'belonging' but for older children who are learning to read, this can also be security in the knowledge that there is a page or two in the class diary that they can read and enjoy all by themselves.

If any members of staff are reluctant to embrace the idea of diaries the last line of persuasion can always be that they offer excellent evidence of good practice and are a readily available assessment record. But hopefully the children's enjoyment whilst advancing their writing skills will be reason enough to embark on the journal writing journey.

Personal journals –formal and informal

Foundation Stage assessment records are now in the form of profiles based on written and pictorial observations of children's learning. Specialists such as an educational psychologist or speech therapist visiting the setting can get a picture of the child's learning experience before they start to work with the child. Parents can also share these profiles and add their own observations. When children move to a new setting these profiles should go with them so that an easier transition can be facilitated.

It's important for a child to contribute to his or her assessment record and that it's in the form of a personal journal that the child has a sense of ownership over. Try to keep assessment profile journals readily available in the setting so that both you and the children can readily suggest work that can be documented. Encourage children to take photographs to put into their journals as a visual record of their achievements. What goes into the profile should be negotiated as far as possible and each new success that is recorded against the journey towards the Early Learning Goals should be celebrated together as appropriate.

By their very nature, assessment records are formal documents and thus cannot be entirely a child-initiated writing resource. It's a good idea therefore for each child to have an A4 notebook that is entirely their own and can be freely accessed to write in whenever they want to. It's important that an adult has no input into these books; that no piece of mark making is annotated and that the child is not told which page to start on or how to write. Any adult supervision or instruction within these books should only really happen at the child's invitation. It's important that a child has a special place to write where there is no adult intervention or interruption unless the child has requested it.

A collaborative noticeboard

When you invite your children to participate in the upkeep of your setting's noticeboard then you take a giant leap of faith into the world of co-operative writing. You have encouraged unconditional participation and as such must accept with a smile that the notice board may never again be a pristine vision of colour co-coordinated beauty. Please try to overlook any imperfections that appear and look the other way rather than correct or 'tweak' anything that does not seem quite right to your practitioner's perfectionist eye. It's so easy to damage the aspiring writer's confidence. If you feel unable to stop yourself altering and editing then it's better not to have a shared noticeboard, which is a shame because it can be an excellent way of encouraging children, staff and parent/carers to share ownership of their setting and its daily life.

In order to maintain a little order you could divide the board with paper borders and ask the children to help you to write headings such as 'dates to remember', 'items for sale', 'wanted', 'lost and found', 'this week's newsletter' etc.

It's welcoming to add a section for 'special things' where families can share aspects of their culture, religion or family life. This may be a photo of a first communion, a child's Bar mitzvah, Diwali celebrations, the photo announcement of a new baby etc. – all special times to share and talk about are good conversation openers for parents as they drop off and collect their children.

This can also serve as a resource board of fun, inexpensive things to do in your local area for young children and their carers.

You could also have a table under the noticeboard for spontaneous artwork, items of interest that the children have made or found either in your setting or at home. Here everyone can contribute an item with a brief written description if they wish. If parents are busy or in a rush, offer to write the description of the child's 'treasure' with them or find treasures with the children in the setting so that no-one feels excluded by pressure of time.

These activities foster a sense of belonging, not only for your children but also for your staff and for the parent/carers in your setting. It will help to encourage feelings of purpose and belonging as well as involvement in a joint writing project.

There are other types of display boards which encourage group writing. Once again these collaborative writing efforts are fun and may not result in neatly presented boards but they do encourage a sustained writing interest.

To ensure that the boards maintain aspects of child-initiated writing, resources need to be readily available nearby and you need to remind the children of the kinds of things that they could be writing about. When a child has made a model to be proud of, remind them that they could make a name label for it and put it on the display table for everyone to see. Or ask them if they would like to take a photo of their den and label it before they print it out and pin it on the display board.

As children begin to label their own work and contribute to display boards you may find that they extend this ownership by making display banners, signposts, flags and larger labels of welcome. Here are some ideas for collaborative display boards:

Our day at school/nursery

Children can take photos and annotate a typical day, a school outing or special times of the day – particularly useful for children who find transitions difficult to manage.

Annotated picture timetable

During the day ask the children to take photos with you of the different activities that are going on and a photo of the clock showing the time these activities are happening.

Include shots of children entering your setting, carers leaving and then coming back at the end of the session to collect the children and the children finally leaving. Seeing pictures of their family/carers and friends coming back for them and then themselves actually leaving the premises gently reminds homesick children of the natural order of things and that they will soon see familiar faces from home. Ask the children to help download, print and compile these into a picture timetable. This will help children with their writing and mark making skills but also with their pre-reading and reading skills.

Picture timetables encourage children to be aware of the passing of time and how they will be spending this time in your setting. Many children find it comforting to know what will come next rather than to have the next activity suddenly sprung upon them. Similarly, most children find transition times easier to deal with if they have had a little warning. Rather than merely being told it's tidy up time, it seems fairer to warn children that it's time to begin to wind down their game as it will soon be time to tidy up. Offer opportunities to save their models, writing etc to be continued later. Have as little tidying away as possible so that play is disrupted as little as possible and can be returned to and continued.

Joke board

Encourage children to write a joke on a post-it note and stick it on the joke board. As a background to the board have a large laminated child's joke that everybody understands. You will get lots of jokes that aren't jokes, aren't funny, have no punch line and are merely a narrative as your children begin to understand what a joke is, how to remember one and then how to deliver it! And then when they can finally deliver a funny joke you will be inundated with all manner of cheesy old jokes. But that laminated joke will keep you all going in the meantime!

News board

Encourage staff, children, parents and carers to add their own snippets of news: birthdays, new babies, exams passed etc.

'In case I forget' message board

Let the children write memos on a white board near your chair – things you must remember – i.e. letters to go home, or the name of a child leaving early that day or being collected by a different person from usual.

'Memphis says' board

Place a laminated speech bubble next to a picture of a favourite character or a child in the class. Children can then write in the speech bubble what they think the character is saying using whiteboard marker pens. Several of these can offer a storyboard for the children to record conversations that may have taken place in the current chosen stories e.g. The Three Little Pigs, Red Riding Hood etc.

It's fun to draw around a child and have a life size character and then the laminated speech bubble can be large enough to accommodate the children's writing. Put a pocket on the character's clothing to hold the marker pens and a cloth for wiping away the writing, ready for children to independently write in the speech bubble.

Some children are familiar with market research surveys and are generally very interested in what their friends think about things.

Case study

How do you feel today?

The leaders of a nursery attached to a primary school had noticed that children who had previously appeared to be quite settled within the setting were finding it quite difficult to separate from their parents/carers each morning and were becoming tearful. Several parents had disclosed to the nursery nurses that the children were experiencing difficulties at home with parents splitting up. One child had been bereaved whilst several others had recently moved house. It was unusual for so much transition to be occurring at the same time. It was impossible to predict from one day to another how the children were going to be.

The leaders set up a 'How do you feel today?' board and all the nursery children drew a face showing how they were feeling that day – happy, sad, giggly, mischievous (most copied the mischievous face forgetting what it meant but liking the sound of the word!). The staff liked this direct way of asking the children how they were feeling that day and it did work; such was the level of emotion being experienced by these young children.

Gradually the board became a clipboard survey and the children went round asking each other how they felt that day.

Gradually new surveys were carried out:
'What did you have for breakfast?'

'What's your favourite story?'

'What's your favourite dinner?'

'What's your favourite activity in nursery?'

The children loved asking each other questions, enjoyed noting down the answers and the possibilities were seemingly endless. Surveys became a permanent part of the setting's mark making fun.

Weather station survey

Most children love being outdoors in all weathers especially what we as adults would call 'bad' weather. Many children I have taught enjoyed keeping weather records.

Resource ideas for your weather station

- Container to catch and measure rainfall
- Weather vane and windsocks
- Outdoor thermometer
- Indoor barometer
- Weather chart
- Camera
- Weather diary to describe the weather, record rainfall figures and temperature and feature pictures of your setting in different weather conditions and seasons
- Simple non-fiction books about the weather
- Access to online weather forecast

Just as writing is synonymous with mark making and finger painting so writing covers both writing letters and numbers.

Ideas for writing activities involving numbers

- Children can write their own labels for the number of children who can play at any one time in an area e.g. '4 children can play here' with four smiley faces labeled 1,2,3 and 4.
- In surveys, children can add a mark making tally and the final total.
- Show children how to make their own chalked hopscotch frame in the setting's outdoor area.

- Make a chalked number snake outside on the path or a numbered ladder on a wall – this can then be linked to playing a snakes and ladders game outdoors with other activities with a snakes and ladders theme i.e. a snakes and ladders obstacle course.

- An activity course with skipping ropes, hoola hoops, beanbags with a number sign written by the children indicating how many times they must skip, hoola, throw and catch before moving on to the next activity.

- Count how many children are in nursery/school each morning and a different monitor each day records the number.

Taking it further

It's important that children are involved in the routines of your setting's working day. Rather than merely taking the register, dinner numbers, messages to the school office, try to include the children in the actual writing of the note. As writing numbers is often a little ignored, with letter formation seemingly being concentrated on more, this may be a good opportunity for working on number formation and showing why it's so important to form numbers correctly. When the children understand that someone could potentially miss out on a lunch if the school cook cannot read the number correctly, accuracy suddenly seems to take on a new kind of relevance!

Key questions

Every day is a rich writing opportunity. Are we making the most of this daily resource? Accommodating ad hoc writing opportunities is not easy especially in the rush of a hectic day. The following questions may help us to think about incorporatiing more writing opportunities into each day.

- Have we discussed, as a team, the frustrations we may encounter as we explore, with the children, the writing opportunities within our daily routine? Displays, journals and profiles may not be as neat as they once were. Are we comfortable with this?

- Have we discussed the importance of the process of writing as well as the product of that writing not only amongst the teaching team but also with parents and carers?

- Do we encourage and praise the children as they write as well as when they have completed a piece of writing?

- Do we allow the children to decide what and how to write?

- How much of the writing in our setting is child-initiated and how much is adult-directed?

- How much of the writing on display in our setting has been written by an adult and how much by a child?

Personal, Social and Emotional Development

- Respond to significant experiences, showing a range of feelings when appropriate.

- Have a developing awareness of their own needs, views and feelings, and be sensitive to the needs, views and feelings of others.

- Form good relationships with adults and peers.

- Understand that people have different needs, views, cultures and beliefs that need to be treated with respect.

- Understand that they can expect others to treat their needs, views, cultures and beliefs with respect.

Communication, Language and Literacy

- Interact with others, negotiating plans and activities and taking turns in conversation.

- Enjoy listening to and using spoken and written language, and readily turn to it in their play and learning

- Use talk to organise, sequence and clarify thinking, ideas, feelings and events.

- Sustain attentive listening, responding to what they have heard with relevant comments, questions or actions.

- Attempt writing for different purposes,

- Write their own names and other things such as labels and captions, and begin to form simple sentences, sometimes using punctuation.

- Use a pencil and hold it effectively to form recognisable letters, most of which are correctly formed.

Problem Solving, Reasoning and Numeracy

- Say and use number names in order in familiar contexts.

- Recognise numerals 1 to 9.

- Use developing mathematical ideas and methods to solve practical problems.

- Use language such as 'more' or 'less' to compare two numbers.

Knowledge and Understanding of the World

- Find out about, and identify, some features of living things, objects and events they observe.

- Look closely at similarities, differences, patterns and change.

- Ask questions about why things happen and how things work.

- Find out about and identify the uses of everyday technology and use information and communication technology and programmable toys to support their learning.

- Find out about past and present events in their own lives, and in those of their families and other people they know.

- Observe, find out about and identify features in the place they live and the natural world.

- Find out about their environment, and talk about those features they like and dislike.

Physical Development

- Handle tools, objects, construction and malleable materials safely and with increasing control.

Creative Development

- Respond in a variety of ways to what they see, hear, smell, touch and feel.

Maintaining an inviting writing area

'Creative education involves a balance between teaching knowledge and skills, and encouraging innovation.'

DfEE All Our Futures: Creativity, Culture and Education

All settings now have a writing table – an area where the children know that they can readily and independently access a wide variety of stationery and writing implements that will cover all their needs. It's important that this area is monitored each day so that it is always well stocked and attractive. Ideally, it should also be the area where practitioners come for their own writing needs too. Children should know that they need to return items after use and that they need to keep the area tidy so that it is always pleasant and ready to be used by the next person. Ensure that there is a bin for unwanted drafts nearby and that there is a display pin board so that treasured writing can be displayed.

To ensure that interest is maintained try to add new and interesting items each week.

51

Resources to include in the writing area

- A variety of paper – lined, unlined, square, tracing. Offer more coloured paper than white paper as this seems to be more inspiring

- Shaped paper – stars, hearts, alphabets, animals etc. When putting up a display use the off-cuts of backing paper and old backing paper you have recently removed and cut into different shapes – cloud shapes for 'I wish...' writing frames, a smiley mouth for 'I like...' frames etc.

- Printed stationery – either bought cheaply or printed using clipart from your computer and then photocopied

- Pens, pencils, felt tips, crayons, chalks, wax crayons and pastels for resistance 'magic' writing. (To avoid the problem of missing tops from pens you can glue the tops to a piece of wood or along a ruler and then the children simply replace the pen – no searching under the desk for the top. This also avoids the temptation of putting pen tops in their mouths.)

- Paper clips

- Hole punch and treasury tag fasteners

- Stapler

- Diaries, notepads, address books, invitations, greetings cards and postcards

- Stickers, stamps and ink pads

- Raffle ticket books

- Pipe cleaners and plasticine to fashion into letters. These offer writing opportunities and the chance to build finger strength and fine motor skills.

- A magnetic board and letters

- Labels, files and folders.

- Calendars

- A telephone – talking often inspires writing!

- Scissors, glue stick, sellotape, Blu tack and masking tape

- Rulers

- Erasers

- Post box and postage stamps

- Clipboards with pencils attached

- Writing prompts, including name cards, alphabet charts and an invitation to write.

- Make your own writing frames to suit the children's interests and hobbies. Photocopy a relevant picture leaving a small space for writing – small spaces to start with as they are less intimidating to fill!

Try to have a similar area outside or a trolley holding similar resources that can be taken outdoors.

Resources to include in an outside area:

- Artist's studio with easels, books and paintings of famous artists, adult painting media i.e. tubes of watercolours with palette trays as well as the usual children's paints

- Outdoor water painting area

- A place for wax crayon etching

- Floor chalking space

Motivate children to write by having an 'I can write' display board next to your writing table. Take photos of the children writing and add it to the board. It will inspire children to have a go so that they too can have their photo taken and added to the display.

A birthday table

Encourage card making – children can make birthday cards to give to family, pets and friends. They can make bunting and paper hats using scissors and sellotape. Making plasticine cakes will strengthen fingers and encourage fine motor skills. Add birthday cake candles and their tiny holders as this will improve co-ordination and dexterity.

A messy writing table

This is not for the faint hearted! A wipe clean table is needed outdoors or in an area with a wipe clean floor. Add media directly to the table that the children can write directly into with their fingers e.g. finger paints, soap flakes, coffee granules, food colouring, glitter sprinkles or a combination of these things. Make the consistency fairly thick to facilitate easier mark making and less mess!

Extendable writing and writing walls

Some children are fascinated by the extending capability of a roll of lining paper on the floor and will often spend a long time trying to 'fill up' the space with their mark making.

Lining paper can be used on the floor or perhaps the easier option is to secure it to the wall at child height. With this option though, the onus is on you to remind them on a daily basis that it is fine to write on this special 'writing wall' in our setting but it is not appropriate to write on any wallpaper in our own homes or at our grandparent's homes!

Date each new piece of paper and annotate what the children tell you about their mark making, as this will give you an insight into their interests and their growing imagination. Write their names for them if they are unable to do so as this gives them ownership of their work and makes them keen to show visitors as well as family and friends what they have done.

As each piece of lining paper is completed, do not remove it from the wall simply add a fresh layer on top. After several months you will have a comprehensive planning and assessment writing record should anyone ask for one which, no doubt, someone will!

Lining paper rolls are fun to take outdoors though you may want to cut them into more manageable lengths. Again they can be fixed to walls or simply rolled along the ground.

Paper attached to brick walls can be used to take wax crayon rubbings of the brickwork. Similarly, lining paper can be attached to tree trunks, pathways and other textured surfaces to get similar effects. Blackboards, magnetic letter boards, collage boards, whiteboards and interactive whiteboards all offer 'writing wall' opportunities. Care has to be taken that they are at the right height for all your children to access; that writing implements are readily available and that the right pens are used with each board. Mistakes are expensive on interactive boards but this should not stop free independent access.

I know this may sound obvious but never underestimate the use of a coloured paper for livening up an activity that has been used before and may have lost some of its initial impact. Use of a bright lining paper often makes the activity seem like new again and renews interest especially if children are invited to choose the colour.

Key questions

Writing areas can very easily become tired looking and jaded. We need to not only maintain them but to model their use. If we are not inspired to use them, then we can not expect our children to want to use them. The following questions may help us to consider the writing area and its use from our children's point of view.

- Do we have designated mark making/writing areas in our setting – both indoors and outdoors where both adults and children can find all the writing implements they require?

- Are the writing areas easy to access independently?

- Do we have sufficient resources for all stages of writing i.e. different thicknesses of pens, pencils and crayons to accommodate the different stages of fine motor skills and pencil control?

- Do we check each day that dried up felt tips are thrown away and pencils and crayons sharpened?

- Each week do we put something new into the area to sustain interest and motivation?

- Do we ensure that the resources are good quality? Do we include 'real life' resources: diaries, suitable invoices, appropriate letter headings etc.

- Do we take time to sit with the children and enjoy writing with them, modelling how to write, talking about our writing, what we are doing and how we write; so that some of he mystery is taken away?

- Do we allow the children to make their own special occasion cards or are they expected to make a card that we have offered as an example that must be copied?

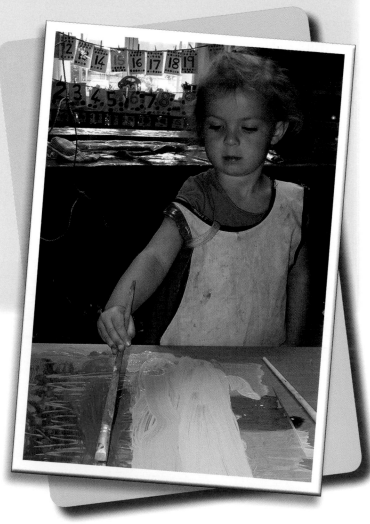

Personal, Social and Emotional Development

- Continue to be interested, excited and motivated to learn.
- Be confident to try new activities, initiate ideas and speak in a familiar group.
- Maintain attention, concentrate, and sit quietly when appropriate.
- Select and use activities and resources independently.

Communication, Language and Literacy

- Interact with others, negotiating plans and activities and taking turns in conversation.
- Enjoy listening to and using spoken and written language, and readily turn to it in their play and learning.
- Extend their vocabulary, exploring the meanings and sounds of new words.
- Use language to imagine and recreate roles and experiences.
- Link sounds to letters, naming and sounding the letters of the alphabet.
- Use their phonic knowledge to write simple regular words and make phonetically plausible attempts at more complex words.
- Explore and experiment with sounds, words and texts.
- Know that print carries meaning and, in English, is read from left to right and top to bottom.
- Attempt writing for different purposes, using features of different forms such as lists, stories and instructions.
- Write their own names and other things such as labels and captions, and begin to form simple sentences, sometimes using punctuation.
- Use a pencil and hold it effectively to form recognisable letters, most of which are correctly formed.

Problem Solving, Reasoning and Numeracy

- Say and use number names in order in familiar contexts.
- Talk about, recognise and recreate simple patterns.
- Use language such as 'greater', 'smaller', 'heavier' or 'lighter' to compare quantities.

- Use language such as 'circle' or 'bigger' to describe the shape and size of solids and flat shapes.
- Use everyday words to describe position.

Knowledge and Understanding of the World

- Investigate objects and materials by using all of their senses as appropriate.
- Look closely at similarities, differences, patterns and change.
- Select the tools and techniques they need to shape, assemble and join materials they are using.

Physical Development

- Handle tools, objects, construction and malleable materials safely and with increasing control.

Creative Development

- Respond in a variety of ways to what they see, hear, smell, touch and feel.
- Express and communicate their ideas, thoughts and feelings by using a widening range of materials, suitable tools, designing and making, and a variety of songs and musical instruments.
- Explore colour, texture, shape, form and space in two or three dimensions.

Writing and creative development

When we work creatively we are able to see connections with things we have learnt before; our children are able to make connections between curriculum areas too. Working creatively also helps us with problem solving. This is invaluable when we are trying to learn something that may not come easily to us or which may need a lot of practice. Many of us, though not all of us, find creative activities pleasurable and even relaxing, which can thus enhance the learning experience.

It would thus seem reasonable to suppose that writing can, and indeed should, be taught alongside the creative development learning area of the Foundation Stage curriculum.

The way to a child's writing heart can be via his or her stomach, though you may only want to encourage this occasionally! Whilst we must all be health conscious and promote healthy living to the children in our care, I think that most practitioners are very aware that our children love their food and love learning that involves the preparation, cooking and eating of that food.

Reluctant readers and writers suddenly become much more interested in reading and writing when food is involved! Reading and writing cooking magazines, cookery books recipe cards, menus, shopping ingredient lists and the preparation for cooking sessions that will actually be carried out, offer reward and incentive.

Cooking sessions need to be carried out soon after the writing preparation as young children will find it difficult to comprehend writing a shopping list for something that will be cooked at a later date, even the following day. Any writing and shopping needs to be done early on in the session so that the food preparation and/or cooking can be completed in the same session, otherwise the child will feel cheated and any incentive will be lost for next time you plan to include writing with a food related activity.

Writing need not be limited to recording menus and recipes. Low fat/low sugar biscuits and cakes could be pre-baked as part of a math's activity teaching volume and capacity, weighing and measuring. In the follow-up session children could ice them with their initials or words that are important to them, using icing pens.

Alphabet and number moulds and cutters could be used to make savoury biscuits and sandwiches for snack time and lunches.

Children can also 'write' using food on a flat surface such as a clean tabletop, an individual tray or large dinner plate. Indeed, children often do this independently anyway at snack time, spelling out their name, their pet's name or initial letters in raisins, breadsticks etc and then relishing eating each letter!

Tubes of cream cheese can be used to 'ice' letters on crackers or slices of toast. Pieces of salad vegetables and fruits can be used for other letters e.g. batons of carrots or celery to represent 'l, t, f' etc., slices of cherry tomatoes to represent the circular movements in the letters 'b, d, p'. Just a little imagination and the fruit and salad bowl can be the entire alphabet!

Edible media can be used for young children to finger paint with, e.g. cream cheese or yoghurt placed in a shallow dish. The colour and smell of these foods appeal to all of the senses and are usually enjoyable experiences for children.

You can also hold food taste tests where a variety of food samples are set out and the children record their favourite foods using simple tick or smiley face charts. This can be linked to healthy food programmes e.g. favourite fruits, vegetables etc.

Enriching the writing process with role-play

In Learning Through Play Tina Bruce discusses how, writing can be enriched by adding play to the activity. 'Encouraging play with writing might seem to take longer and even to waste time, but taking a long term view it leads to a steady and lasting progress.'

There should always be writing opportunities in the role-play area that are subject linked to the role-play scenario – jotter pads for lists, phone message boards, clipboards, registers, diaries, address books, etc.

As well as the role-play area that links with the planned topic, I always had a teacher's role-play area next to my chair where we gathered for music time, story time and home time. Here I kept a basket with a register for the children to play with, a pen, some story books, stickers for 'the teacher' to reward their pupils, mini whiteboard and marker pens, a story for story time, 'Notes for parents' which 'the teacher' can write. The children knew this was their basket to play with and that they could climb on to my chair and be the teacher – beware you may see yourself through your children's eyes!

However, this was also a good way to see what they were learning as they often rehearsed learning situations we had been previously practicing such as reading, writing or counting techniques. Any misconceptions could be noted by staff and addressed sympathetically there and then. Sometimes, so as not to break the flow of play, we made a note in our planning to address them in our whole group sessions soon afterwards.

Adding writing opportunities to favourite activities

Children often offer a commentary as they play, telling you what they are doing, talking to the other children or the toys involved in their play. Sometimes this is a way of controlling their play and explaining the rules of their play to the other children. Sometimes this commentary is copying what they might have seen in other areas of their lives – in television sports commentary for instance. Without interfering with the flow of play these commentaries can be successfully recorded by the children.

Provide a 'Goal Score' blackboard and chalks in a football area together with microphone for a 'Match of the Day' type commentary. This could be extended for older children with a match report for the class delivered from a cardboard box television screen? For written sports journalism, children can record their races and games with photos and writing.

Put a clipboard in the pet area so children can write feeding instructions, log when they fed the animals or add a note for the next person who feeds them.

Put together lengths of fabric to wrap and drape as clothes as well as the usual dressing up ensemble. Include sewing pattern books. Encourage children to draw their designs. Would the children enjoy drawing simple patterns for doll's clothes which they can then make? Simple T shapes make good tops for action figures and baby dolls alike and rectangles make hats and scarves. Fabric pens can be used to decorate fabric swatches as well as T-shirts, T-towels, etc. Paper dolls with paper clothes could also be made and decorated.

A roll of lining paper and pens in the construction area allows the children to make their own car mats, road maps, farms and train tracks.

When they are involved in a cooking activity, children can write a recipe or menu card and a taste test card with smiley faces or sad faces indicating whether the resulting food is tasty enough to cook again.

Children often enjoy visiting the school office and many office staff enjoy their visits too. 'Helping in the nursery office' can be a fun activity if office staff enjoy having a small group of young visitors. This works well if children are given small tasks which involve writing during their visit. Children can then set up a role-play school office. If you are working from your own home can you encourage children to take a note for you – shopping you may need when items are used up at snack time or a note about a phone call received?

Letter writing

As children become more accustomed to writing and when they are also forming opinions about favourite book and television characters you might like to add simple letter writing frames to your writing table. A picture of their favourite character with 'Dear ...' on a piece of writing paper will often inspire a letter or two.

I realised how fascinated my children were by letter writing when a child in our class was poorly and we wrote to her. Her mother encouraged her to write back. Letters happily bobbed back and forth and this quickly became our most popular activity and child-initiated at that! When the child returned, I was concerned how I could maintain all that spontaneous writing. This child's absence had opened my eyes to how much the children had enjoyed letter writing.

Case study

On a small table I set up a small letter writing tray with paper, envelopes, sticker 'stamps', assorted pens and felt tips and together we made a letter box in which we could 'post' our letters. On a walk to our letter box at the end of the road we noticed that letters were collected at certain times of the day and we decided on set collection and delivery times for our own letter box. The children took it in turns to be post person setting up their own rota on a clipboard and ticking their name off when they had had a turn. All of this they managed to self-direct after the first couple of adult assisted turns.

When practitioners were out and about at weekends we began to pop a postcard in the letter box wherever we were. If we forgot, we printed a photo of the place we had visited (sometimes from the internet) on to card and made it into a postcard and posted that, sometimes via Royal Mail in the box at the end of the street and sometimes in our nursery box. The logistics didn't really matter – the children just loved getting a letter, reading something that was written especially for them and more importantly these postcards inspired them and their parents to send postcards to nursery when they were on their travels. These could be from our local town, when they visited the nearby theme park or the town's castle!

Writing to music

'Being creative enables children to make connections between one area of learning and another and so extend their understanding.'

Curriculum Guidance for the Foundation Stage. QCA

Background music in a classroom is calming for both practitioner and child. However, it can also be used as a prop for writing –inspiring fluency for free flow mark making when practicing pen control is one of your learning intentions and simply enjoying the large movements that can be made and the fun that can be had. As the tone, beat and rhythm of a piece changes so can the marks being made and each crescendo can create a collage of different writing marks and styles. Even reluctant writers can get quite carried away, offering prolific pieces of work while enjoying this relaxed writing form.

Cover a table with paper and the children can collect their favourite mark making equipment. They can then mark make/write in time to the music of a favourite tape. You could also write to music by mark making with finger paints on the table and then pressing the finished design on to large sheets of lining paper.

Ideas for music you could use

- A nursery rhyme tape i.e. drawing the Grand Duke of York and his men marching up and down the hill or Humpty Dumpty sitting on his wall etc.

- Classical music allows for more spontaneous mark making in time to the music. You can choose whether or not you offer any explanation of the music title e.g. Korsakov's The Flight of the Bumble Bee or Prokofiev's Peter and The Wolf.

- Favourite character theme tunes could also be used or favourite seasonal songs.

Writing our own books

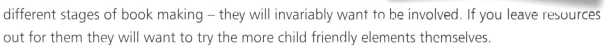

From the very first day children arrive in our settings we share books with them. It seems reasonable to me that very soon after we should begin to make our own books and share those at story time too.

When children see you taking photos, annotating them, sticking them together, laminating the book – all the different stages of book making – they will invariably want to be involved. If you leave resources out for them they will want to try the more child friendly elements themselves.

If you show you welcome their lead they will be happy to ask you to help with the more adult necessary aspects such as laminating.

Books can be about anything and everything:

- Our own version of a favourite book.

- A big book of the people in our setting.

- A class diary of our day.

- A 'working' class diary with dates to remember such as outings, visitors, birthdays etc. Ask children to add to these each day.

- A class trip.

- Where we live – an address book with photos of our houses, pictures of local shops, library, bus stop, school etc.

- Our school/nursery book – showing the children's annotated photographs.

- 'Things I like in the nursery' book with photos and annotations.

- Our birthday book – dates of birthdays, the birthday person and how you celebrate a birthday in your setting.

- Our pets.

- High frequency word books – for older children. As you teach the high frequency words, make books themed around this weeks high frequency word practice e.g. 'I am'. Help the children to take photos of each other and write 'I am' and their name with their photo on each page. Have the book on display in the reading area. You will find children reading this independently.

It is a huge morale booster for a child beginning to read to find a whole book they can read by themselves. They may also try to recreate this book at the writing table again because success is assured. Have some blank paper books ready assembled for the children to complete if they wish. You could write other high frequency big books with the children such as 'I like…' 'I can…' 'Look, here is…' By introducing a big book with children's names into familiar areas of your setting, suddenly reading seems easier and is fun as children look for their friends in the pictures rather than reading scheme characters who can sometimes seem a little remote.

● Special interest books are also fun to make. Non-fiction books about our hobbies, interests, pets etc. are personal to us and possibly more interesting and relevant to read and may engage some of our usually less interested readers and writers.

Children love to hear stories where they are the main characters. They can help to write these stories and take photographs of themselves to illustrate the book.

They can also make up their own stories using storyboards and story boxes (shoes boxes with story puppets and props) and you can help compile these stories by acting as their scribe and taking photographs.

Children find it easier to write stories if they have played a part in story telling – making up and acting out stories of their own. We can help to record these stories and to make them into exciting big books, which the children will enjoy helping to write and later read.

Making books

Children may want to make their own books. Have some folded paper on your writing table propped up with a label inviting the children to make a book. Offer a prop sample with stickers of a favourite book character and a simply written page. A piece of paper folded over is a good start as there is less blank paper to fill – no writer's block to overcome at the first attempt!

Concertina books are fun. These can be the standard rectangular concertina books but these can also be cut into shapes e.g. boys and girls holding hands in a line ready for mark making.

Children recognize the initial letter in their name early on in their reading and writing so will enjoy a book that has their initial letter on the front cover or a book in the shape of the letter. Simply cut out the letter in several differently coloured pieces of paper and staple them together either at the left hand side or at the top to make a flip-over book.

Later, and for older children, have a selection of home made books ready to be filled on your writing tables. Folded and stapled paper makes an instant ready to use book as does a strip of paper folded concertina style. Gradually children will simply make their own books up anyway but these simple ready made books will give them a start. Again, don't include too many blank pages as this may be a little off-putting.

Taking it further

By the middle of the reception year many children will be able to write a sentence or two independently. The thrill of being able to do this usually inspires children to write more.

Encourage more independent writing with a writing wall. Laminate high frequency words and place them, in groups, in labelled pockets attached to your writing wall. Children learn to read the words before they learn to spell them. So they will recognize the word and will then be able to use the laminated card to use the word in their writing. I added laminated adjectives held together by a key ring – big , little, tall, small with a self- explanatory picture and font sizing. I also had similar key rings holding laminated colour names – the font matching the colour name so yellow written in a yellow font etc.

Encourage the children to write in 'golden sentences'. A 'golden sentence' has to have a capital letter at the beginning of the sentence, a full stop at the end, a doing word (verb) and a describing word (adjective). I used both the words and explanations verb/doing word and adjective/describing words. Offer rewards such as house points, golden time or whatever your reward system is when elements of a golden sentence are used. Obviously, children will take a lot of time to write complete golden sentences so just one element deserves reward I used to say one house point for each element and five additional house points for a complete golden sentence. These children were in the Spring/ Summer term of the Reception year.

The writing wall also had a large golden sentence which the children had 'marked' with ticks, smiley faces, house points and 'well done' stickers so they knew what they were looking for when writing their own golden sentence.

After a little explanation the children were able to use the writing wall independently.

Key questions

Many of us learn more if our learning is within a creative context, yet many of us claim not to be creative! The following questions will help us to reflect upon how we consider our own and other's creativity, how that links to learning and how we can convey that to others.

- Have we considered sufficiently, as a team, how children can develop their writing skills via creativity? Are we confident in expressing this knowledge to the children's parents and carers?

- Do we place as much importance on the process as we do on the end product?

- Do we consider particular colleagues as being 'the crafty, arty or creative ones' and consequently designate them to be the ones to plan and lead creative activities? Similarly, are some colleagues designated as being more suited to planning and leading 'more academic' subjects such as writing or number skills?

- Do we consider some children to be more creative than others?

- Do we have a restricted view of what is creative?

- How much autonomy do we allow children within the area of creativity? Do the children make decisions about what materials to use? Do we interfere too much? Are we concerned if something does not look like an accurate representation?

- When creativity is not tidy do we feel uncomfortable?

- Does a writing activity have to be a quiet and tidy activity?

Links with Early Learning Goals

Personal, Social and Emotional Development

- Continue to be interested, excited and motivated to learn.

- Be confident to try new activities, initiate ideas and speak in a familiar group.

- Maintain attention, concentrate, and sit quietly when appropriate.

- Respond to significant experiences, showing a range of feelings when appropriate.

- Have a developing awareness of their own needs, views and feelings, and be sensitive to the needs, views and feelings of others.

- Have a developing respect for their own cultures and beliefs and those of other people.

- Form good relationships with adults and peers.

- Work as part of a group or class, taking turns and sharing fairly, understanding that there needs to be agreed values and codes of behaviour for groups of people, including adults and children, to work together harmoniously.

- Understand what is right, what is wrong and why.

- Consider the consequences of their words and actions for themselves and others.

- Dress and undress independently and manage their own personal hygiene.

- Select and use activities and resources independently.

- Understand that people have different needs, views, cultures and beliefs that need to be treated with respect.

- Understand that they can expect others to treat their needs, views, cultures and beliefs with respect.

Communication, Language and Literacy

- Interact with others, negotiating plans and activities and taking turns in conversation.

- Enjoy listening to and using spoken and written language, and readily turn to it in their play and learning.

- Sustain attentive listening, responding to what they have heard with relevant comments, questions or actions.

- Listen with enjoyment, and respond to stories, songs and other music, rhymes and poems and make up their own stories, songs, rhymes and poems.

- Extend their vocabulary, exploring the meanings and sounds of new words.

- Speak clearly and audibly with confidence and control and show awareness of the listener.

- Use language to imagine and recreate roles and experiences.

- Use talk to organise, sequence and clarify thinking, ideas, feelings and events.

- Hear and say sounds in words in the order in which they occur.

- Link sounds to letters, naming and sounding the letters of the alphabet.

- Use their phonic knowledge to write simple regular words and make phonetically plausible attempts at more complex words.

- Explore and experiment with sounds, words and texts.

- Retell narratives in the correct sequence, drawing on language patterns of stories.

- Read a range of familiar and common words independently.

- Know that print carries meaning and, in English, is read from left to right and top to bottom.

- Show an understanding of how information can be found in non-fiction texts to answer questions about where, who, why and how.

- Attempt writing for different purposes, using features of different forms such as lists, stories and instructions.

- Write their own names and other things such as labels and captions, and begin to form simple sentences, sometimes using punctuation.

- Use a pencil and hold it effectively to form recognisable letters, most of which are correctly formed.

Problem Solving, Reasoning and Numeracy

- Say and use number names in order in familiar contexts.

- Count reliably up to ten everyday objects.

- Recognise numerals 1 to 9.

- Use developing mathematical ideas and methods to solve practical problems.

- In practical activities and discussion, begin to use the vocabulary involved in adding and subtracting.

- Use language such as 'more' or 'less' to compare two numbers.

- Find one more or one less than a number from one to ten.

- Use language such as 'greater', 'smaller', 'heavier' or 'lighter' to compare quantities.

- Talk about, recognise and recreate simple patterns.

- Use language such as 'circle' or 'bigger' to describe the shape and size of solids and flat shapes.

- Use everyday words to describe position.

Knowledge and Understanding of the World

- Investigate objects and materials by using all of their senses as appropriate.
- Find out about, and identify, some features of living things, objects and events they observe.
- Look closely at similarities, differences, patterns and change.
- Ask questions about why things happen and how things work.
- Build and construct with a wide range of objects, selecting appropriate resources and adapting their work where necessary.
- Select the tools and techniques they need to shape, assemble and join materials they are using.
- Find out about and identify the uses of everyday technology and use information and communication technology to support their learning.
- Find out about past and present events in their own lives, and in those of their families and other people they know.

Physical Development

- Move with confidence, imagination and in safety.
- Move with control and coordination.
- Recognise the importance of keeping healthy, and those things which contribute to this.
- Handle tools, objects, construction and malleable materials safely and with increasing control.

Creative Development

- Respond in a variety of ways to what they see, hear, smell, touch and feel.
- Express and communicate their ideas, thoughts and feelings by using a widening range of materials, suitable tools, imaginative and role-play, movement, designing and making, and a variety of songs and musical instruments.
- Explore colour, texture, shape, form and space in two or three dimensions.
- Recognise and explore how sounds can be changed, sing simple songs from memory, recognise repeated sounds and sound patterns and match movements to music.
- Use their imagination in art and design, music, dance, imaginative and role-play and stories.

Conclusion

Learning to write does take a long time. In order to maintain our children's enthusiasm and to encourage writing to be a child-initiated activity we need to continue to introduce new and exciting writing activities, which continue to surprise and offer 'wow' factor whilst meeting learning intentions. This in turn helps us, their teachers, to maintain our own enthusiasm to teach our children the wonderful skill that is writing.

Good luck and enjoy!

Further reading

Bayley Ros & Featherstone Sally	**(2010) Child-initiated Learning**	Featherstone/A&C Black
Bilton, Helen	**(2000) Playing Outside**	David Fulton Publishers
Bruce, Tina	**(2004) Developing Learning in Early Childhood**	Sage Publications
Clere, Lynn	**(2004) The Little Book of Bags, Boxes and Trays**	Featherstone/A&C Black
DfES/QCA	**(2000) Curriculum Guidance for the Foundation Stage**	DfES
Hall, Nigel (Ed)	**(1989) Writing with Reason**	1989 Hodder Arnold H&S
Hall, Nigel & Robinson, Anne	**(1995) Looking at Literacy**	David Fulton Publishers
Lewisham (LEARN)	**(2002) A Place to Learn**	available from eys.advisors@lewisham.gov.uk
Roberts, Ann	**(2002) The Little Book of Props for Writing**	Featherstone/A&C Black
Campbell, Helen	**(2002) The Little Book of Writing**	Featherstone/A&C Black
Clarke, Jenni & Sally Featherstone	**(2008) Young boys and their writing**	Featherstone/A&C Black